Miraculous Magic Tricks

MENTAL MAGIC

by Thomas Canavan
Illustrations by David Mostyn

WINDMILL
BOOKS

New York

Published in 2014 by Windmill Books, an Imprint of Rosen Publishing
29 East 21st Street, New York, NY 10010

First Edition

Author: Thomas Canavan
Editors: Patience Coster and Joe Harris
US Editor: Joshua Shadowens
Illustrations: David Mostyn
Design: Emma Randall

Library of Congress Cataloging-in-Publication Data

Canavan, Thomas, 1956–
 Mental magic / by Thomas Canavan.
    pages cm. — (Miraculous magic tricks)
 Includes index.
 ISBN 978-1-4777-9065-6 — ISBN 978-1-4777-9066-3 (pbk.) —
 ISBN 978-1-4777-9067-0
 1. Magic tricks—Juvenile literature. I. Title.
 GV1548.C225 2014
 793.8—dc23
                          2013021321

Printed in the USA

CPSIA Compliance Information: Batch # BW14WM: For further information contact Windmill Books, New York, New York at 1-866-478-0556
SL003848US

CONTENTS

INTRODUCTION

Within these pages you will discover great magic tricks that are easy to do and impressive to watch.

To be a successful magician, you will need to practice the tricks in private before you perform them in front of an audience. An excellent way to practice is in front of a mirror, since you can watch the magic happen before your own eyes.

When performing, you must speak clearly, slowly, and loudly enough for everyone to hear. But never tell the audience what's going to happen.

Remember to "watch your angles." This means being careful about where your spectators are standing or sitting when you are performing. The best place is directly in front of you.

Never tell the secret of how the trick is done. If someone asks, just say: "It's magic!"

THE MAGICIAN'S PLEDGE

I promise not to reveal the secrets of magic to those who are not magicians.

I promise to practice these magic tricks over and over again before attempting to perform them in front of an audience.

I promise to respect my art, the art of magic.

MIND-READING

1 Prior to the trick, the magician chooses an assistant who will be in on it. The magician tells the assistant the trick depends on him clenching and unclenching his teeth, so that his face muscles tighten and relax. The magician rehearses placing his hands on the assistant's temples—the soft bits at the side of the forehead.

2 To perform the trick, the magician asks for a volunteer from the audience to help him with a mind-reading trick. He picks the secret assistant.

3 The magician says he will leave the room. Before he goes, he asks the other spectators to write down a four-digit number, show it to the assistant, and then hide the paper.

4 The magician leaves the room while the spectators do this, then he returns to face the assistant.

5 The magician looks the assistant in the eye, then raises his hands to the assistant's face so that they cover his cheeks. The magician's middle fingertips should lightly touch each temple.

6 The magician says he will read the assistant's mind to learn the secret number. The assistant clenches his teeth and the magician counts the number of clenches. In this way, the assistant signals the four digits that were written on the paper. He pauses after each set of clenches. So, for the number 5478 he clenches five times, then four, then seven, then eight.

7 Slowly the magician takes his hands away from the assistant's head. He closes his eyes as if imagining the number, then speaks it out loud to the stunned audience!

MATCHING ANSWERS

ILLUSION
The magician predicts the answers a spectator will give to a set of five questions.

1 The magician places ten small pieces of paper, two pencils, and two mugs on a table. Then he asks for a volunteer from the audience.

2 He gives the volunteer five pieces of paper, a pencil, and a mug. The magician keeps the rest for himself.

3 The magician says he will ask the volunteer five simple questions. He tells the volunteer to write each of her answers, with its number, on a slip of paper. Then he asks her to fold the paper and place it in the mug. The magician says he will write his predictions on his five pieces of paper. He will try to match the volunteer's answers.

4 Each question is simple enough to have a one-word answer. The first could be, "What city would you like to visit?"

SUMMER

5 The volunteer writes down her answer and puts the paper into the mug. The magician writes "summer" on a piece of paper and puts it into his mug.

6 When both papers are in the mugs, the magician asks the volunteer what her first answer was. Let's imagine that the volunteer says "Rome."

7 Now the magician asks his second question, which could be: "What is your favorite flower?" The volunteer writes down her answer and puts the paper into the mug. The magician writes "Rome" on a piece of paper and puts it into his mug.

8 The trick continues like this. Each time, the magician writes down the volunteer's answer to the previous question.

9 The magician's final question is: "Which season do you like best?" As the volunteer writes down her answer, which is most likely to be "summer," the magician writes down the volunteer's fourth answer. The magician asks another volunteer to read out both sets of answers. They match!

COIN DETECTOR

1 Prior to the trick, the magician makes sure his magic table is covered with a cloth with a bold, colorful pattern.

2 Next the magician plucks out one of his hairs and sticks it onto one side of a coin with a piece of clear tape. He trims the hair so that it extends beyond the edge of the coin by about half the coin's width. He puts the coin in his pocket.

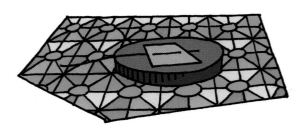

3 To perform the trick, the magician casually reaches into his pocket and pulls out the coin he has prepared. He puts it on the table.

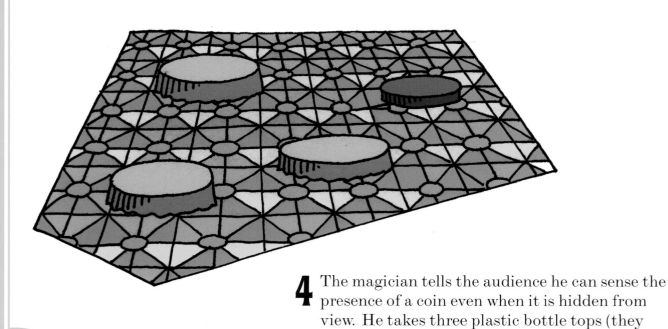

4 The magician tells the audience he can sense the presence of a coin even when it is hidden from view. He takes three plastic bottle tops (they should be opaque, not clear, and slightly wider than the coin). He places them next to the coin.

5 The magician covers the coin with one of the bottle tops and places the other two tops on either side. "Right," he says, "the coin is under this top." He uncovers the coin—and the spectators laugh or groan!

6 "But I can do more," says the magician. He asks the spectators to slide the tops around on the table and line them up again—in any order—while his back is turned.

7 When the spectators have finished, the magician turns round to face them. He examines the tops—staring, sniffing and even listening to them. What he's really doing is looking for the tiny bit of hair sticking out.

8 Once he's sure, the magician picks up the top and reveals the coin underneath. Ta-dah!

SHOW ME YOUR MIND!

ILLUSION

A volunteer is asked to write down a series of important years and other numbers. He is then told to add them together. The magician guesses the sum exactly.

1 The magician chooses a volunteer and gives him a piece of paper and a pencil.

2 The magician turns his back to the volunteer and asks him to write down the answers to four questions. Each answer should be written directly beneath the previous one.

17

3 First, the magician asks: "What year were you born?" Then he asks: "In which year did something important happen to you?" The third question is: "How many years ago did that big event happen?" And the final question is: "What will your age be at the end of this year?"

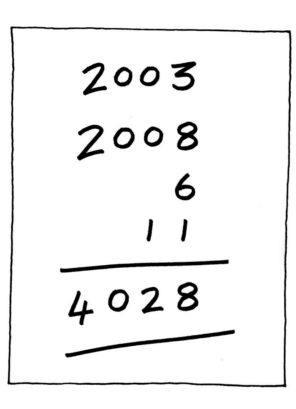

2003
2008
    6
  11
―――
4028

4 Now the magician asks the volunteer to add up the four numbers.

5 While the volunteer is doing this, the magician thinks of the current year and doubles that number in his head.

6 The magician turns and tells the audience the number he has just calculated. Then he asks the volunteer to show his "secret number." They're the same!

X-RAY VISION

1 The magician places the following props on a table: a small piece of paper, a felt-tip pen, a small brown envelope, a slightly larger white envelope, and a piece of dark construction paper.

2 He asks for a volunteer to come up to the table. The magician stands behind the spectators, with his back to them.

20

3 He asks the volunteer to write a short word on the piece of paper, using the felt-tip pen.

4 The magician asks the volunteer to place the paper in the brown envelope and then to slip the brown envelope into the white envelope.

5 The magician asks the volunteer to hold up the white envelope so that the audience can see it. He asks the audience if they can read the word written inside. They can't.

6 The magician says: "It's now safe for me to turn round." He looks at the envelope. He can't read the word either.

7 "I need to make an X-ray telescope," he says. He folds the construction paper in half and tears along the fold to make two strips.

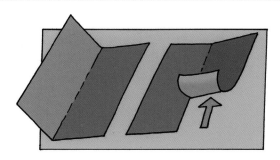

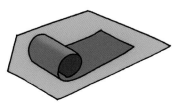

8 The magician rolls up one strip to make a small tube. He holds it to his eye, like a telescope, and picks up the white envelope.

9 With the "X-ray telescope" touching the envelope, the magician can read the word hidden inside!

MAGIC TIP!
THE TUBE BLOCKS REFLECTED LIGHT FROM THE WHITE ENVELOPE, MAKING IT EASIER TO SEE THE WORD ON THE PAPER INSIDE.

THE COUNT OF SIX

1 Prior to the trick, the magician finds six small objects to use as props—sweets, crayons, paper clips, or anything he can hold easily.

ILLUSION

The magician seems able to predict which object a volunteer will pick from a group of six.

2 He finds a blank card (about twice the size of a playing card) and a felt-tip pen.

3 To perform the trick, the magician stands behind a table with the six objects, card, and pen in front of him. He tells the audience that he will use these props to read a volunteer's mind.

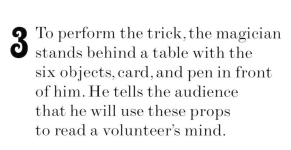

4 He holds up the objects one by one, counting out one to six as he does so. He places the objects back down in no particular order—not in a straight line.

5 The magician asks a volunteer to come up and examine the objects. The volunteer chooses an object, but does not reveal which one it is.

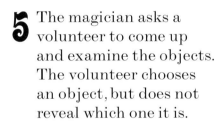

6 The magician says he has read the volunteer's mind and knows the chosen object. He writes a number between 1 and 6 on the card and places it face down on the table.

7 He rearranges the objects a little to distract the audience and asks the volunteer to point to his chosen object. The magician says, "Right, he has chosen object number X" (the number he has already written on the card.)

MAGIC TIP!
THIS TRICK RELIES ON THE POWER OF SUGGESTION. IT'S BEST TO USE SIX SIMILAR OBJECTS SO THE SPECTATORS ARE LESS LIKELY TO LINK EACH NUMBER TO A PARTICULAR ITEM.

8 Then the magician says: "And the number I predicted was . . ." and he flips over the card. It's the same number!

AND THE YEAR IS ...

1 Prior to the trick, the magician gathers together about ten or twelve coins. They should be of different value, but all from the same year. He puts them in his pocket.

2 To perform the trick, the magician asks for a volunteer from the audience. When the volunteer joins him, the magician turns his head away and reaches into his pocket for the coins. He makes it clear that he cannot see the coins in his hand. He asks the volunteer to pick one and look at it carefully.

3 The magician says he can tell by the coin's mysterious force what year it was made. The magician calls out the date and asks the volunteer to show the coin to the other spectators. It's the same year!

1993

1993

1993

STOP THE PULSE!

1 Prior to the trick, the magician stuffs a pair of socks into his right armpit. He lowers his arm to keep the socks from falling down.

ILLUSION

ILLUSION

The magician says he has learned the ancient trick of making his heart stop when he tells it to. Then he proves it to a volunteer!

2 He invites a volunteer to join him. The magician tells the audience that he will stop his heart and that the volunteer will be his witness.

3 The magician holds out his right arm, taking care to keep the socks in place. He explains he is making it easier for the volunteer to take his pulse, on the inside of his wrist. He asks the volunteer to take his pulse. The volunteer puts her fingertips against the inside of the magician's wrist. When she finds the magician's pulse, she announces it to the audience.

4 "Now," the magician says, "I will use my ancient powers to stop my heart. When I raise my left hand, the volunteer will test my pulse once more." The magician presses his right arm firmly against his body so the socks are tightly lodged. After about ten seconds, he raises his left hand. The volunteer puts her fingers to the magician's wrist. There's no pulse—no sign of a beating heart!

CRAZY CRAYONS

1 The magician places a box of eight crayons on the table. He asks the spectators to examine them to make sure they've not been marked or tampered with.

ILLUSION

Behind the magician's back, the spectators choose a crayon from a boxful. The magician is mysteriously able to pick it out from the rest.

2 The magician turns his back to the table, folding his hands behind him, and asks a spectator to pick a crayon and put it into his right hand.

3 Holding the crayon behind him, the magician turns to face the audience. With the crayon now hidden from view, he scrapes off a tiny bit of wax with his thumbnail.

4 The magician turns away again so the spectator can take the crayon and put it back in the box. The magician folds his hands in front of him and turns round. He puts his hands up to his head "to help concentrate." As he does so, he secretly notes the colour of the crayon wax under his thumbnail.

5 Now he examines the crayon box. He opens it slowly, decides which crayon matches the thumbnail wax, and pulls it out of the box.

FURTHER READING

Barnhart, Norm. *Amazing Magic Tricks.* Mankato, MN: Capstone Press, 2009.

Cassidy, John and Michael Stroud. *Klutz Book of Magic.* Palo Alto, CA: Klutz Press, 2006.

Gardner, Martin. *Mental Magic: Surefire Tricks to Amaze Your Friends.* Mineola, NY: Dover Publications, 2010.

Klingel, Cynthia and Robert B. Noyed. *Card Tricks.* Games Around the World. Mankato, MN: Compass Point Books, 2002.

Tremaine, Jon. *Instant Magic.* Hauppauge, NY: Barron's Educational Series, 2009.

WEBSITES

For web resources related to the subject of this book, go to: www.windmillbooks.com/weblinks and select this book's title.

GLOSSARY

digit (DIH-jit) A character that represents part of a number. For example, the number 37 is made up of two digits: "3" and "7."

opaque (oh-PAYK) Impossible to see through. The opposite of transparent.

pulse (PULS) The rhythmic pushing of blood around a body.

tamper (TAM-puhr) To make changes to an object without letting anyone know.

temple (TEM-puhl) The flat part of the head between the eyebrow, ear, and hairline.

X-rays (EKS-rayz) Invisible beams of light that can pass through solid objects.

INDEX